Connecticut

BY MARI KESSELRING

Published by The Child's World®
1980 Lookout Drive • Mankato, MN 56003-1705
800-599-READ • www.childsworld.com

ACKNOWLEDGMENTS
The Child's World®: Mary Berendes, Publishing Director
The Design Lab: Design and production
Red Line Editorial: Editorial direction

PHOTO CREDITS: Ross Tracy/Fotolia, cover, 1, 3; Matt Kania/Map Hero, Inc., 4, 5; Laura Stone/Shutterstock Images, 7; iStockphoto, 9, 10; Jill Lang/Shutterstock Images, 11; Keith Muratori/Shutterstock Images, 13, North Wind Pictures/Photolibrary, 15; AP Images, 17; Matt Sayles/AP Images, 19; Jeffrey M. Frank/Shutterstock Images, 21; One Mile Up, 22; Quarter-dollar coin image from the United States Mint, 22

LIBRARY OF CONGRESS CATALOGING-IN-PUBLICATION DATA
Kesselring, Mari.
Connecticut / by Mari Kesselring.
p. cm.
Includes bibliographical references and index.
ISBN 978-1-60253-451-3 (library bound : alk. paper)
1. Connecticut—Juvenile literature. I. Title.

F94.3.K48 2010
974.6—dc22

2010016169

Printed in the United States of America in Mankato, Minnesota.
July 2010
F11538

On the cover: Morgan Point Light is an old **lighthouse** near Noank, Connecticut.

CONTENTS

Geography

Let's explore Connecticut! Connecticut is in the northeast United States. This area is called New England. Connecticut is the third-smallest state in the country. Connecticut's southern border is Long Island **Sound**. This waterway flows into the Atlantic Ocean.

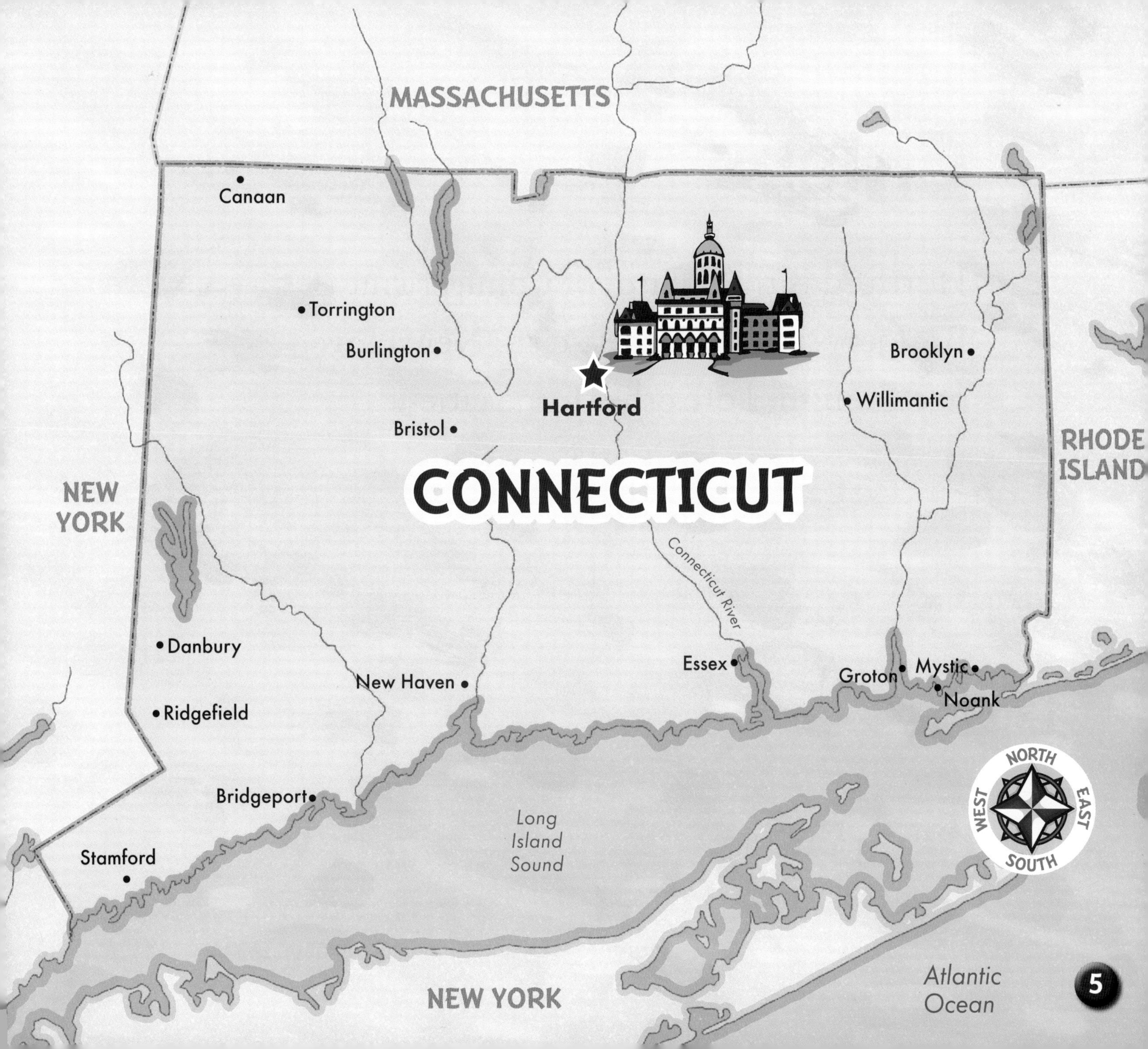
MASSACHUSETTS
Canaan
Torrington
Burlington
Bristol
Hartford
Brooklyn
Willimantic
RHODE ISLAND
NEW YORK
CONNECTICUT
Connecticut River
Danbury
Ridgefield
New Haven
Essex
Groton
Mystic
Noank
Bridgeport
Stamford
Long Island Sound
NORTH
EAST
SOUTH
WEST
NEW YORK
Atlantic Ocean

Cities

Hartford is the capital of Connecticut. Bridgeport is the largest city. New Haven and Stamford are other large cities.

Hartford is by the Connecticut River. ▶

Land

Connecticut has rocky areas dotted with lakes and rivers. Near the ocean are some valleys and beaches. Connecticut also has flat land for farming.

Five Mile Point Lighthouse in New Haven used to warn ships of dangerous rocks. ▶

Plants and Animals

Forests cover about one-third of Connecticut. The state tree is the white oak. It has gray **bark**. The Connecticut state bird is the robin. It is brown with a red chest. Many robins live in Connecticut all year, even in winter. The mountain laurel is the state flower. It has white and pink **petals**.

The mountain laurel opens in late spring and early summer. ▶

People and Work

More than 3 million people live in the small state of Connecticut. Many people in Connecticut work in factories. **Manufacturing** is important in this state. Other people in Connecticut work for **insurance** companies.

A power plant provides jobs for people in Bridgeport. ▶

History

Native Americans were the first people to live in the Connecticut area. In 1633, people from Europe began moving to the area. It became a **colony** owned by England. During the **American Revolution**, people in the area fought to be free from England. Connecticut became the fifth state on January 9, 1788.

Men in Connecticut signed up to fight during the American Revolution.

GENTLEMEN
ADVENTURERS
WAX
QUEUE

Ways of Life

Many people in Connecticut enjoy spending time outdoors. Sports such as ice hockey and basketball are **popular** in the state. Many people also value the rich history of the state.

Many people in Connecticut enjoy watching college basketball. ▶

UCONN
21

Famous People

Actors Katharine Hepburn, Meg Ryan, and Glenn Close were born in Connecticut. Eli Whitney was born here, too. He invented the cotton gin. Author Stephenie Meyer was also born in Connecticut.

Stephenie Meyer wrote The Twilight Saga. ▶

Famous Places

Many people visit Connecticut in the fall to see the colorful trees. Connecticut also has many historic places. These include old houses, such as the home of author Mark Twain.

Mark Twain's home is in Hartford. ▶

State Symbols

Seal

The three plants on the Connecticut state seal are grapevines. Go to childsworld.com/links for a link to Connecticut's state Web site, where you can get a firsthand look at the state seal.

Flag

The words in the Latin language on the Connecticut state flag mean "He who transplants still sustains." This is the state **motto**.

Quarter

The Charter Oak is on the Connecticut state quarter. It stands for freedom. The quarter came out in 1999.

Glossary

American Revolution (uh-MER-ih-kin rev-uh-LOO-shun): During the American Revolution, from 1775 to 1783, the 13 American colonies fought against Britain for their independence. Some battles of the American Revolution were fought in Connecticut.

bark (BARK): Bark is the covering on a tree trunk. The white oak has gray bark.

colony (KOL-uh-nee): A colony is an area of land that is newly settled and is controlled by a government of another land. Connecticut was once a colony owned by England.

insurance (in-SHUR-unss): Insurance is something people can buy to help them with money in case of an accident. Many people in Connecticut work at insurance companies.

lighthouse (LYT-howss): A lighthouse is a tall building near an ocean or large lake that uses lights to warn ships of danger. Five Mile Point Lighthouse is in New Haven, Connecticut.

manufacturing (man-yuh-FAK-chur-ing): Manufacturing is the task of making items with machines. Manufacturing is an important business in Connecticut.

motto (MOT-oh): A motto is a sentence that states what people stand for or believe. The Connecticut motto is "He who transplanted still sustains."

petals (PET-ulz): Petals are the colorful parts of flowers. The mountain laurel has pink and white petals.

popular (POP-yuh-lur): To be popular is to be enjoyed by many people. Ice hockey and basketball are popular in Connecticut.

seal (SEEL): A seal is a symbol a state uses for government business. The Connecticut seal has grapevines on it.

sound (SOWND): A sound is a narrow body of water between a mainland and an island or peninsula. Connecticut's southern border is Long Island Sound.

symbols (SIM-bulz): Symbols are pictures or things that stand for something else. The state seal and flag are Connecticut's symbols.

Further Information

Books

Evento, Susan. *Connecticut*. New York: Children's Press, 2004.

Furstinger, Nancy. *Connecticut*. New York: Children's Press, 2008.

Grodin, Elissa. *N is for Nutmeg: A Connecticut Alphabet*. Chelsea, MI: Sleeping Bear Press, 2003.

Web Sites

Visit our Web site for links about Connecticut: *childsworld.com/links*

Note to Parents, Teachers, and Librarians: We routinely verify our Web links to make sure they are safe and active sites. So encourage your readers to check them out!

Index